The Compass

The Journey to Success

Table of Contents

Introduction

Conclusion

Acknowledgments

Spiritual intelligence also helps us discern true principles that are part of our conscience, which are symbolized by the compass. The compass is an excellent physical metaphor for principles, because it always points north. The key to maintaining high moral authority is to continually follow "true north" principles.

-Stephen R. Covey, *from his book* The 8th Habit

Introduction

In these days and times, there is a significant challenge ahead for black men to not only survive but to thrive in the 21st century. For black men to mentor and share their love for younger generations of African Americans, we must sacrifice for the greater good of our community.

I began thinking about this book while in College at Saint Augustine's in Raleigh, NC in the spring of 2005. A product of Oakland, California, I was tired of hearing about the peers who I grew up with being buried and leaving a legacy of death on the streets for their younger family members and neighbors.

One summer, I had an internship at KTVU television station. For this reason, I was always drawn to watching this network, even while I was away. While watching KTVU one day, it hit me, and I was taken aback by all the black on black violence and senseless crimes occurring every week back home. It seemed as though not a day went by that there was not another murder in the City of Oakland. I decided I wanted to do something to help my community after college. After I graduated from Saint Augustine's College, I went back to Oakland to do my part or at least what I perceived to be my part in my young, ambitious heart. My quest to "help" turned out to be an adventure I was not prepared to handle.

The journey started with me going into Oakland area public schools. I had an opportunity to talk to young boys and girls about a variety of topics. I talked about life skills and showed films to help drive the point about why it was wrong to kill another black person. My primary goal was to transform lives in the midst of the despair experienced in my community. My desire was to get my fraternity and others involved in the process. Many of the fraternity members were involved in other projects in our chapter and their time was focused in other areas.

The one fraternity brother who assisted me was Renaldo Blocker, a doctoral student who attended the University of Wisconsin. We sat down at a seafood restaurant and discussed strategies for helping the community. We decided to do a focus tour to educate youth on the value of attending Historically Black Colleges and Universities (HBCU) and the reasons why African Americans from California should visit and consider attending those institutions. We set up appointments at several schools in the Oakland area.

As days passed, it was more and more clear to me that my community was losing too many black men to homicides. I became more passionate about doing my part to assist in uplifting them as much as I could. This book is about my journey. It tells the good, the bad, and the ugly, and I hope it will result in young people in communities such as mine doing something about our present state. The alarm has sounded.

Chapter 1
Kappa and Mentors

In my younger days, while playing baseball in the Oakland
Babe Ruth league for the Kappa baseball team, I had valuable
experiences. This was in the late 1980's early 1990's. Although I did
not understand the depth of it back then, I consider myself blessed as I
reflect on the experience. I interacted with individuals like Bob
Maynard, the African American owner of the Oakland Tribune. He was
a pioneer. He owned the Tribune from the late 1980's to the time of his
death in the spring of 1993. I saw in him an opportunity to have the
more elegant things in life and the diligence to work hard and be a
confident leader in the community.

I played baseball with Bob Maynard's son, Alex. We went on
to play in the first Oakland Babe Ruth Championship in 1992. We
played against our rivals, Allen Temple Baptist Church. While we lost
the championship game, getting to the final match was exciting. We
learned many great lessons along the way. It was a humbling
experience interacting with gentlemen like Bob Maynard. He gave me

hope as a young kid, and I realized then, I could accomplish anything with faith and courage. He worked alongside the Mayor of Oakland at the time, Elihu Harris. Mr. Harris and my father were fraternity brothers. I would later grow up and join the same fraternity.

While in high school and college, I focused on my communication skills. I majored in Communications in college and would go on to work with the local Major League Baseball team as a cameraman. I also worked for my college radio station, WAUG and hosted a show.

Growing up, I was inspired and influenced by Elihu Harris. It was great to see a black man become the mayor of my city during my lifetime. Elihu would come around sometimes to the Kappa baseball games. I was delighted to see him and talking to him made me feel proud. It took me years to realize the impact of having successful mentors around and how they influenced and shaped my life. Another great influencer was Robert L. Harris. He was a lawyer for Pacific Gas and Exchange (PG&E) in California and held the office of Grand Polemarch (President) of Kappa Alpha Psi Fraternity, Incorporated in the 1990's. As a kid, I would travel with my father and mother to Kappa conventions and I heard Robert speak many times. He was always professional, inspiring, and seemed very powerful. As a young man, I wanted to reach the level of power Robert had attained.

The man I owe my respect to is my father Stephen McClendon. He was an awesome mentor in my life. He would take my mother and me on trips all around the country to Kappa conventions. Those were the best times for me. As a kid, I was in the room with people like Johnnie Cochran, an excellent lawyer who helped to free Hall of Fame football player O.J. Simpson. I also remember former Mayor of Los Angeles, Tom Bradley, and Congressman Mervyn Dymally from Los Angeles, and Reginald Lewis, a businessman from New York. Being around these great men gave me the confidence I needed to realize I could accomplish anything as an African American man.

My father was the General Manager of my Kappa baseball teams. We would get new uniforms every year. I would, of course, have a say in picking out the uniforms for the team. I played for the Kappa youth baseball team from the age of 5 up until I was 15 years old and he coached me all the way through.

My father showed me the ins and outs of running a baseball program as well as how to relate to kids from different parts of town. Many of the kids from West Oakland had different home structures than mine. Many were socioeconomically disadvantaged. I played

9

baseball with a lot of players from broken families. They didn't always have someone there to cheer them on. Looking back, I am very fortunate and blessed that I have a mother and father who genuinely cared about me and worked hard to keep me out of trouble.

The majority of the Kappa men I met in my life helped me in some capacity. Men like Dr. Ed Wilson who guided me through the process of getting into college when I desired to get out of Oakland. Men like Johnnie Cochran who demonstrated the importance of working and helping the people who need you most.

When I think back, my mentors helped strengthen me, shape my character, and develop the persistence it has taken to achieve excellence. As I separated from the shores of my youth and moved into adulthood, I knew I was a recipient of a childhood that was fun, exciting and a blessing. Many other Kappa coaches such as Ralph Grant, a Certified Public Accountant taught me how to be professional and respectful. A great coach who worked with Chevron Oil, Huey Malone, made me a great ball player. He took time to teach me how to play the game with more efficiency. My other coaches were Gary Reed and Mike McCree, who taught me how to locate the ball like Willie Mays in the outfield. My mentors helped encourage me to be a young professional. These Kappa men are distinguished, spiritual and men of strength, courage, and achievement. These men shaped my life.

Mike was the youngest of the coaches. He played baseball at Michigan State. He taught me to work hard, never give up, and be tough. I played on all-star teams that traveled to Canada and Las Vegas and became an all-City baseball player in the city of Oakland in 1999.

In one instance when I was 12, Mike and I were at a Kappa convention in Long Beach, California. We were playing catch on the Long Beach Grand Prix Raceway and I learned a solemn lesson. I was playing catch with him, and for some reason, I was overthrowing the ball. He passionately corrected me and said to me "Either do something with great accuracy or don't attempt to do it at all." Those words hurt me but from that day forward, I decided to challenge myself and grow even more with greater effort in school, baseball, and life.

Wil Ash was also influential in my young life as far as baseball. He was a Certified Public Accountant and worked in a beautiful area of Oakland called Lake Merritt or "Grand Lake." It was and still is a lovely sight to see. Wil would never let up on me. He was always stern and made sure I knew the game of baseball.

Wil's son, Johnny, went on to be an all-star baseball player at Bishop O'Dowd High School. It is a private school in Oakland. He then went on to Stanford University to obtain his degree and then played Minor League ball for the Astros. Johnny has always flourished in baseball.

During my time playing youth baseball, many of the players went on to colleges like Prairie View A&M, Stanford, U.C. Berkeley, Saint Augustine's College, Shaw University, Jackson State University and other state colleges in California.

Many of our players were productive in their lives, but some did not make it and were killed or went to jail. Overall though, the baseball program helped many young black men survive in the Oakland area. I am grateful to be one who survived. I am grateful for the sacrifice these gentlemen made for me and other youth in Oakland.

Chapter 2
Learning Techniques for Young Boys

Learning about one's heritage should be the first thing a young African American boy does. We should read the history of significant black figures to our young boys. When young boys understand who they are, there is a sense of pride and strength that will make them love themselves. Sharing their heritage with them will inspire self-love and help to stop the violence. Positive images are created by the words read to them. When you educate and teach them their heritage, you are nurturing and cultivating a young prince to survive in this harsh world.

Young boys should read books outside of the classroom. These days, the schools' curriculum does not teach black history adequately or accurately. Our young boys must know the writings of Carter G. Woodson, the great historian who created a new education dynamic to teach African American children. The speeches of Frederick Douglass inspired and challenged the horrors of the slave conditions here in America. The history of Malcolm X and how he developed into the prolific African American Muslim leader of his generation; fighting the myths of false narratives against African American men. Children should learn about Father Dusable, the African American fur trader who founded the great City of Chicago. Or better yet, Farrah Gray who at eight years old was a millionaire and did not use his living environment to halt his trajectory of the vast wealth he obtained. If they can learn about their history, there would be no need to worry about them killing themselves. Self-love and appreciation must start at conception.

Once a child knows what can be achieved, there is no stopping him from great success; no matter what the circumstance. The libraries are a great, accessible place to take your child. Reading is essential to help young African American boys think beyond what television displays. A child should be limited to how much television they watch and what they can watch. Make sure the images are positive because children tend to act out what they see on TV.

On another note, please be very careful about the people you allow to be around your child. Think of people who would be a positive influence in your child's life. These relationships can leave lasting impressions and can affect your child's life forever. Utilize the churches for positive impact and mentors. Many of them have computers and different tools and resources for how to learn.

My perspective is the earlier this education starts, the better the child will be equipped to create a successful, healthy life. Math should be a priority and worked two to three grade levels in advance. Get flashcards or use computer technology to get your child into a habit of learning. Utilize tutors at community non-profits and always stay positive and push your child to be the best. Kids learn fast.

For young African American boys, sports are an excellent way for them to learn how to overcome the challenges that life will bring. Never let your child quit a competition if they are playing unless he is injured. Stopping can create an adverse effect for years to come. Sports are a learning tool and this will benefit them as adults. Sports help the children develop character and follow through on commitments. It also teaches them not to give up on themselves. Start kids out in sports young so that they can learn early on how to deal with others. It is good for the growth and socialization of children.

Young boys should not have toy weapons around them. They should not learn to be violent so early; it just gets worse with time. Teach young boys about the world and God. Teach them about positive thinking, faith, and sacrifice. Explain to them why it is essential to stay away from drugs and its distribution. Show them the pitfalls of going to jail and the reason that the United States wants to make money off of disadvantaged children.

Traveling outside of where you reside is excellent for your children, whether riding the train or catching a plane or even going downtown to look at the buildings, is a unique adventure and provides exposure to new things. The problem for some of our kids is we become isolated by circumstances in our community. If we leave and see the beauty outside of our community, it opens up our imagination to strive for endless possibilities.

There should be a plan for education every year as your child progresses through school. Take a close look at what your child brings home. Have teacher meetings and use technology to communicate with your child's teacher via e-mail or phone conference as your schedule permits.

In school, participate in your son's school programs as much as you can. Get family members involved if you cannot carry the load. It takes a village to raise a young child. The child should be required to read a book or magazine on African American history every week. Invoke thought and growth in your son about issues that affect his life. Have a schedule on the wall to teach your son the best use time. Time management is the key to success in your child and also explains structure.

Teach your sons how to use money wisely. I've always believed in the philosophy of needs versus wants. When you go after what you need, rather than what you want, you usually save yourself a lot of money.

Your sons must know financial principles and discipline. Young black men need to understand self-control to survive in this environment. Young black men should learn about college at a young age. It is essential for the survival our young princes. In order for them to be successful, they must develop a plan for school and for post-graduation. We must prepare these young men to be husbands and protectors of their communities and to become productive black men, not just what the world thinks they should be.

If your child is having trouble in school and complains about the teacher, investigate it and don't just brush it off. In essence, the child is not an adult, and there could be countless reasons behind a young child's concerns. Some teachers already have a stereotype that young African American boys are hyperactive and cannot focus, so they treat them differently. They label them early on. Keep a close eye on your young son. Inadequate information and energy can destroy a child's confidence.

When I was young, a teacher who happened to be Asian did not encourage me to be better at math. She told me I was not smart enough to do a math problem. That was a severe shock to me as a young man, and although I told my parents, they felt "the teacher is always right" and she lied to my parents in the parent-teacher conference. My math skills could have been better but my lack of confidence and the lack of understanding from the math teacher were not helpful.

Listen to your children; they could be telling the truth. You know what is best for your son. Schools have a set curriculum that has failed our sons for years. The teachers seem too eager to put our kids in remedial classes. You must at least give your child a chance to survive in the world. Even if your child is at a private school, your child still must be monitored because the school's philosophies could be different from yours.

Chapter 3
Black Men in America

Racism is, unfortunately, a part of my life. As a black man, I can see it all around but as a child, I did not understand racism quite as clearly as I do now. At a young age, I went to a theme park in Northern California with Prescott Elementary School. My mother worked at the school. It was a summer field trip and I was so excited to go. We were an all-black group mainly from the West Oakland area.

When we entered, I overheard a Caucasian lady saying to her friend "We have to wait for all of these niggers to get into the park." I was shocked. I didn't know what to do. I was hurt. It opened my eyes to the harshness of some of the ignorance in our sometimes dark world. From that day on, my life changed. I felt I had to be an excellent representative for my race.

In 1994, I was playing football for the Oakland Dynamites. We were playing in the playoffs against a team called the Vallejo Generals. The Vallejo team was a majority African American team as were we. The league scheduled both organizations to play in a town called Dixon. Dixon is about 45 minutes from Oakland and 30 minutes from Vallejo. It was an all-white town that both the Vallejo Generals and our team clobbered in the regular season.

19

At that time, California was having the worst rain of the early 1990's. After the game, we were muddy, tired, sore, and had lost to the Vallejo Generals 35-7. Like any team, we just wanted a nice shower to warm up and clean off, but an older Caucasian maintenance worker at the field said we couldn't take a shower.

The players were distraught. We could not believe this man would have the audacity to say such a thing. My father, who was the general manager of the Dynamites, was so pissed off. He said, "If this were a white team, you would have let them use the shower." The guy comes up with the explanation that the showers were not working. Many of the kids' parents were angry and very sad. I later found out that some players caught a cold since they didn't put on dry clothing.

As a High School senior playing football at Jon C. Fremont, located in East Oakland, I received a scholarship offer to attend Prairie View A&M University. Many of the Pac-10 schools and top division one schools did not recruit me. This was my only option. At the time, getting out of Oakland had been a dream of mine for a very long time. Many athletes, even close friends of mine, left the city and never came back. It was an attempt to escape the homicides and poverty, an effort to save their own lives.

Playing sports seemed like the only option at the time because the educational structure in certain parts of low-income neighborhoods in Oakland lacked modern educational components to help drive students forward to a successful life. There was no way we could compete in a global economy or work for companies in Silicon Valley. Though the schools were diverse, that was their only advantage. Many of the Oakland schools looked like prisons and created an image of lost hope. The kids model what they see and can be uninspired by their surroundings that are far from beautiful. This was contrary to the other high school campuses in surrounding suburban cities in the Bay Area.

In Oakland, I was an all-city baseball player. It seemed as if the collegiate schools were very biased towards African American baseball players on the west coast. I returned from my first college Prairie View A&M University in Texas having lost my scholarship due to my immaturity and not realizing the level of blessings and responsibilities I had in my hand. I partied and didn't work out as hard as I needed to in order to be great. I had a lack of focus, too much drinking, smoking weed, and chasing women. This all led to my demise and the loss of my scholarship. I left Texas after losing my football scholarship in 2000. I returned home to Oakland and had to be very humble about the forfeited opportunity. I decided to attend a local Junior College in the Bay Area in order to keep the momentum going.

There was a coach from Oregon who previously coached in the suburbs of the bay area in a city called San Ramon. From the onset, I could tell he had a problem dealing with African American players. I encountered racist, biased behavior from my football coaches worse than I'd ever expected to face in the year 2000. As a player from Prairie View A&M University, I thought I was worthy of playing football and hoped to get a scholarship at another school. However, my Hawaiian defensive back coach stated that HBCU's were substandard schools. This made me feel inferior and demoralized. I didn't believe someone would think something so harsh and to openly voice it, left me in disbelief. He often promoted and allowed the Caucasian players to start any chance he could especially during critical games.

I remember a time in particular when a coach of the opposing Junior college team was taunting our coach before the game. He stated his team would throw for over 350 yards on us. In reality, we lost to that team. They threw for more than 450 yards, beating us mercilessly. During that game, our coach still refused to play the African American players. The season was very different from any football season I had ever experienced. At the beginning of the season, the coach told me there would be an equal balance of playing time but the fact is that he gave the African American players less time than the white players.

I distinctly recall that the African American players started mostly during the second half of the game after the team was already in a deficit because they wanted to use us to come back and win. The ones who could have helped the team win, sat on the bench at the beginning of the game. That season, we wound lost seven games out of ten games and ended with a 3-7 record. Most of that coaching staff got fired the very next season.

There is discrimination in many sports. I moved on to pursue baseball again. I was playing baseball at a local junior college. I decided to give ball another shot since I was stellar in high school. I tried out for the local junior college baseball team. The coach seemed to always refer to the Oakland ballplayers as not focused and lacking the fundamentals. This was directed towards the African American team members in a narrow-minded way racially charged way. I told him that there were a lot of good ballplayers that came from Oakland; Frank Robinson, Joe Morgan, Hall of fame player Jimmy Rollins, but he said the players he gets were not fundamentally ready to play College baseball. I proceeded to persevere through the circumstances and show revered leadership for the other black

23

ballplayers and prove this coach wrong for his misinformed statements. I had not played baseball since high school, which was two years prior and it was an adjustment.

We started the season with about ten African American players. Some of the players had kids and jobs so they could not make it in time to the practices. The coach tells the team one day at a meeting that you either decide baseball is your job or you can't play on this team. After that situation, many players quit because their family comes first. So the coach got rid of many African American ballplayers with this mind control tactic.

Secondly, there were players from Alameda, a suburb which is predominantly white, and other cities such as Albany, Fremont, and Concord and a few players from Hawaii. So the coach's objective was to open more slots for his Mexican and Caucasian players and put token few in the outfield or back up if they need them. So, the coach was promoting Hispanic and Caucasian players; showing no appreciation for the African American players. There was a fundraiser where we had to sell ten shirts and three sweaters, which was a requirement if you wanted to play on the team. When September 11 happened, my cousin was working and living in New York. I was shocked and worried, so I decided not to go to the practice. The coach gave me an ultimatum. He told me I would be suspended for the remainder of fall ball unless I sold the college T-shirts and the sweaters. I continued to go to practice because that is what he allows me to do. I get home and ask my mom if she could purchase the shirts, and we would sell them to the family. I sold the merchandise and brought the money to the coach; the team had a game that day. All I wanted to do was to play and show him African American athletes are disciplined, and my skills are better than other players on the teams.

The coach was shocked I brought the money back in a couple of days' time. I asked him if I could play he said no because now it is too late in the season. I felt a rush of blood in my body. I told the coach, "You gave me your word that I would play if I sold the shirts at this time." I said, "Coach, this is not right. Many of the African American ballplayers who came up through the Oakland Babe Ruth League are not given a fair chance to be evaluated. "You are disrespecting many of the players who came through Oakland."

The coach says, "You will still be able to play after fall baseball." I said, "That is unacceptable." I left his office and proceeded to walk to the administration and tell the college administration of the situation. The coach came running after me and told me I could play in the intrasquad game that week. That was not good enough, so I told him I was done playing. I took the coach his shirts and sweaters back and asked for the money back from the fundraiser. The coach agreed to give me back the money.

In a way, I felt redeemed. I played my last game as if my life depended on it. I gave it my all and didn't care if I had to be carted off that field. I was on the inter-squad team that went against the returning players. I was the leadoff batter on the other team. The day I started off with a single and stole second and third and singled in. We went up 4-1 going into the last inning we lost by two points in that game. I scored two points and proved I was a good player. I walked away from that dark misty evening at the College and did not say goodbye. I just knew I had to let it go. I knew the coach would not change.

I changed schools and went on to another College for the spring semester and then proceeded to Saint Augustine's College in the fall semester of 2002. That particular college team went on to win only four games and next season six games. The challenge made me focus and realize that perception is important to never give in to stereotypes and prejudice and hold my head high as an African American black man.

There was another situation in my philosophy class with a white professor. We were talking about African American history.

During a lecture, she said, "African American people did not do anything to enhance American history." I had never been that insulted in my life. I was compelled to explain the many achievements of African American people and how we contributed to the blueprint of Washington D.C and founded Chicago. She was very negative and told me to leave the class. That was another traumatic experience for me.

Another incident I found appalling happened when I worked for a professional baseball team in the bay area. The season started in April and I wasn't allowed on the camera until June. I was already under intense pressure, trying not to make a mistake because I knew that the manager was very condensing. As a young, ambitious college student, I challenged him. One hot summer game in 2006, I was working for the in-house camera operations team. I was positioning the camera and talking to the producers. As I was filming one particular shot, the radio frequency was full of static. I was trying to confirm a promotional piece. I had to position myself for a shoot in order to be visible on the big screen monitors. The producer, who was very opinionated yelled, "Can you speak English properly?" The issue was not my English speaking, it was the headset I was using. I was shocked as I speak proper English very well. His ignorance saddened me but I was determined to endure. I was determined to complete the assignment and not quit. That position was the most humbling job I had ever had. Every day I worked for this professional baseball team, I felt like I was a victim of 'working while black.' My skin was my sin and some people were determined to make my time there challenging.

Sadly this was 2006. My naivety would not allow me to believe this was real life, especially in the bay area. I had to experience this for myself. It was my wake-up call. When I worked the camera I didn't receive any help from any of the other workers. I had on to teach myself techniques. They told me to just sit in the music producer's booth the whole game but I was determined to make a difference. On July 5, 2006, I had to deal with another issue. This one was on me, sort of. When I got to work that day, the control room the manager and another cameraman cornered me. The manager yells, "Intern has to go home." I was embarrassed in front of the whole staff. The problem was that I had worn a Deion Sanders shirt. Deion Sanders was a two-sport athlete in the early 1990's who played for the Atlanta Braves and Atlanta Falcons. He also happened to be my favorite player on the planet. I admired him and modeled some of my sports ambition after him. I understood there was a policy that we were not to wear any t-shirts that represented another sports organization. I just didn't think about it when I got dressed that day. They said, "Go home and change." I responded very calmly, "You guys were supposed to give us team t-shirts at the beginning of the internship, and that never happened." They didn't respond to my statement.

I went home crying, telling my mother what happened. She was upset. I put another shirt on and went back to work. I walked up to one of the managers who cornered me and said: "Is this ok?" He looked at me and responded, "Yes." I went back to work and I was fine the rest of the day. That wasn't it. At the beginning of the season, the manager put me on the calendar to frequently work the games. During the summer, I worked the majority of the games while other interns went on vacations. In August, there were only a couple of weeks left in the Major league schedule. At this time, the manager changed the schedule and stopped putting me on the schedule towards the end of the season. I was not in the lineup for any of the playoff games. I was distraught. Other interns got preferential treatment over me in some ways. They seemed to get a lot more camera operating time than I did during the entire internship and some eventually got full-time jobs with the organization.

The Saint Mary's students had to go back to school at the latter part of August because the fall semester was starting. Unfortunately, they were getting all the games I wasn't getting emails for those games.

Instead, I had to call the manager repeatedly to find out my schedule. One day, I was at my girlfriend's house and we were planning our day together. The manager called me just two hours before the game and told me he needed me to come into work. Usually, when they scheduled you, they would let you know early in the morning. I expressed my frustration to my girlfriend. My time was getting cut shorter and shorter. They were showing me that my time with them would not help advance my career with the team. My last time working as a cameraman was in September. I only worked a couple games. I also worked the final game of the season against their rival. The team made it to the playoffs that year, but I was not invited to work any of the playoff games.

After the season was over, I never received my check. I called another intern, who was also African American, to ask if he'd received his check. He said he had. The last word I received from the organization was that we would be paid by November. I called the Human Resources director to ask about it and the manager put me on speaker phone with the director of interns. The director claimed that I had been promoting myself with sports anchors and a local affiliate of Fox Sports. The fact is, I knew those anchors from working as an intern for them a couple years before. I told the director I did not need to promote myself. Although I did not self- promoting, there was no policy stating we could not advocate for ourselves. I felt the director was trying to find any reason not to pay me for the internship. I reminded the human resources manager that I had been a diligent worker the entire season.

I felt this stemmed from the dispute with the other manager. I ran down the list of why I was a good worker and how the other interns from the local college were doing more self-promoting than me. After listening to me, they said they would call me back. I proceeded to write a detailed list of the incidents that occurred and sent it to the human resource director and the manager, along with a note saying that I deserved compensation for my work.

About a week later, they called back saying they are only going to pay me half of my internship money. I was appalled. I had worked the entire season and deserved my pay. My father told me to go to the Bureau of Labor Statistics and file a grievance. I followed his advice and went downtown at once.

As I approached the counter, there was a Hispanic lady who was very impolite towards me. There was a paper to be filled out about the loss wage grievance. I had already downloaded it and completed it prior to my arrival. On the paper, it had a section where you could document times and hours worked for the week. I told the lady I just wrote out precisely the situation and just needed to complete one more part in order for it to be complete. The lady kept cutting me off. I called the director of this department who was in San Francisco and she told me exactly what needed to be done. I followed her directions and turned in the form.

As I continued to tell the lady at the counter exactly what my grievance was about, she cut me off. I attempted to talk to the lady, but she ignored me and said she was going to call security on me. I was feeling anxious to get this resolved and get my money. I left feeling humiliated. I walked downstairs to call my father. I told him what happened and I was agitated by this treatment. He told me to calm down and go back upstairs and talk to her again. I went back upstairs and there were still people in the room. As I walked into the office the lady, again being abrasive, tells me she is going to get her manager and have her witness the exchange between the two of us. The lady proceeds to bring another lady to see me so I tell the new woman that I would like to see a manager. Finally, she gets someone else to speak to me. I told her my situation, and she took the paperwork. She gave me a date to come back and see the judge and settle my case. After spending two and a half hours there, I learned a valuable lesson that day. It is

32

always good to follow up and stay focused on what you want to get accomplished. I went back about 2 months later. I met with the baseball organization. I won my case and I was paid for the whole internship.

Chapter 4
The Black College Experience

The first black colleges and universities I visited were in Tennessee. I went to Fisk University and Tennessee State and Meharry Medical College. My parents took me to visit these colleges. I did not know much about the schools. I just thought they were lower level schools compared to what I have seen on television.

I was impressed by the structure of the college. I could feel the presence of pride and history. I would sometimes watch Eddie Robinson and the Grambling State Tigers play Southern University on television for the annual Bayou Classic. Besides that, I did not know much about black colleges. My sister Kim went to Morris Brown in Atlanta and she had a challenging experience in at college. She finished her years with a lesson that taught her about struggle and how challenging it can be to earn a degree. The experience she went through inspired me to appreciate black colleges.

I also learned about Tennessee State University when I was in elementary school. I was Wilma Rudolph for a celebration of phenomenal women. Yes, I actually portrayed Wilma in a school production. I watched the Wilma Rudolph story and appreciated her story; no other school would take her before she broke many records. I also knew about Walter Payton. He was the Chicago Bears great who is still one of the top ten running backs in NFL history. He went to Jackson State University in Jackson, Mississippi. Lastly, I followed NFL great Jerry Rice's career. He attended Mississippi Valley State University. He is currently in the Hall of Fame. I was so impressed by these black college football players.

In my young life, I did not think about attending a black college seriously until my senior year in high school. I was interested in many different colleges like Oklahoma State and the University of Washington. They did not recruit me. Only Prairie View A&M University gave me a chance. When I did not get a football scholarship to some of these major universities, Prairie View gave me a one-year renewable scholarship. I was introduced to Prairie View by my football coach, Matthew Walker, who played at Prairie View and graduated from there. I commend him for his sacrifice and love. I thank him for taking young, black men out of Oakland and help them with an opportunity to succeed in life.

When I went for a visit to see Prairie View for the first time in spring 1999, I was amazed because it was in the country, about 50 miles outside of Houston, Texas. I never thought I would attend there.

35

The coach saw my film, and I received a scholarship to attend Prairie View. At the school, I met a lot of beautiful black people. I was thinking, "Wow a campus for us." The dorms were big and it was the last year they were going to have the dorms.

The school was remodeling all of the dorms to accommodate new apartment-style dorms for freshman. I missed out on that luxury but the experience I had was well worth it. I had many teachers who worked with me to make sure that I knew how to write well and think about subjects. My favorite classes were debate and sociology. I also took a Communications course since that was my primary major. We would discuss the black college experience and how it is perfect for black men.

The men who come from various places around the United States to challenge themselves at black colleges benefit from the curriculum. They build character, achievement, and a sense of pride. Professors challenge you to do your best and work with you to become a better student. At a majority white college, you may run into philosophical differences that can extend your stay in some cases. There are different situations for each student. Black colleges are there to give us a chance to succeed. They were created after slavery to develop and promote industrial or service types of jobs from 1860's to

36

early 1900's. The colleges are ideal for black men in inner cities because they can attend a college and get a degree and be exposed to others from places different than where they grew up. This is a better alternative than staying on the block in the neighborhood where killings and other mayhem is quite possibly the norm.

African Americans have a hard time getting into the prominent universities unless they get high grades in high school and can receive a scholarship. Sometimes, it helps if we go to private schools and cultivate our academic skills. HBCU's are not all the same. There are some colleges that more prominent than others. You will find a school that is suitable to fit your needs.

The colleges are always growing. The dorms of HBCU's are being modernized in some capacities. This is beneficial so they can accommodate the students' needs. You will find a melting pot of wealth at these black colleges. You will find students from all over the United States, Caribbean islands, and even students from Europe and South America. The experience is great for challenging oneself on an academic level. The students will have a fair chance of succeeding because they can meet their professor and will not be just a number.

The classroom experience is engaging and the environment ensures the knowledge is rooted. Some people expect the financial aid process to be faster. They expect just a bank transaction. I've also heard people say it's faster at schools like N.C. State or LSU or U.C. Berkeley. They brag that some of these institutions are better when it comes to getting their package of financial assistance and also brag about having better facilities. Well, in essence, the black colleges are improving their facilities. The HBCU's have improved greatly over the past decade. Have patience with the process of growth for those colleges. The black college is a family of students focused on earning a degree and striving for success in life.

The bands and the football games are lively and very exciting. A black college football game is an event. The events start with barbeques, also known as tailgating in other sectors. These barbeques have all kinds of southern cuisine and it tastes so good. Then, the battle of the bands is a must. There is dancing and the crowd gets really into it. The bands are in sequence. Each black college band has their significant flavor of style. The more traditional bands cannot stand up to black bands. These bands at our HBCU's have been getting down for years. The battle of the bands is an actual event. It is held in New Orleans at the Mercedes Benz Dome. The top ten black college bands get selected to battle each other. The event is filled with great music and procession of the musicianship of the bands.

38

The Fraternity life is fascinating at HBCU's. They have a sense of a history, brotherhood, and achievement. They also have cool parties at times. There are movies depicting Fraternity life at HBCU's. Movies like "School Daze" and "Stomp the Yard" go in depth about the purpose of black fraternities and their purpose and the process in which one is initiated to join. The fraternities are good places for black men to enter social groups and gain a sense of working together as a unit.

The black college experience is a chance for black men to grow and leave the community of distractions and a chance to find a new perspective in their lives. The HBCU's have a great history that will help the young men see others who came before them and looked like them. If they could do it, so can we. The black college experience is an excellent experience.

Chapter 5
Know Your History

In our 400 plus year journey of toil and achievement, living in the land initially of the Native American, we have marked a story for the ages in history. We have built this country. We made and constructed the white house. Our history helped cultivate the layout of what is now Washington D.C. We built and designed the University of North Carolina at Chapel Hill and Duke University and were not invited to the ceremonies on the campuses. We were the first to die in the revolutionary war; a man of courage and high integrity, Crispus Attucks. We were some of the most courageous journalists in the land. Ida B. Wells reported on lynchings and risked her own life. Our young men must learn their history from teachers, parents, pastors, politicians, fraternities, and community leaders.

They must understand that rap music was positive once upon a time in the 1980's. It is important to know that some entertainers from the past used their voice to wake up their people. The godfather of soul, James Brown, woke up people with his song, "Say it Loud, I'm Black and I'm Proud." Booker T. Washington built an institution for young African Americans to see their greatness and potential. They had a vision for themselves beyond the local drugs and penal system. The great mind of Marcus Garvey cultivated the minds of black men and women to unify and grow economically. With great courage and strength, we will make a significant difference. The great Dr. King showed that God would bless you if you sacrifice for your people. Malcolm X taught us that we must stand up, fight, and self-educate as it is essential for survival.

Learn your history and your people. Learn about black people and the trials and tribulations they went through to obtain an education and start fellowships. Read about W.E.B Dubois and his challenge with the NAACP. Read about Frederick Douglass and how he taught himself to read and write with productive energy. When you learn about African American history, it gives you strength wisdom and courage to continue in your life and accomplish great things.

In the history of African Americans, whenever faced with an obstacle the individual never stopped believing in themselves and their purpose and their focus on God. We were freed from bondage because of religion and substance. Harriet Tubman led the Underground Railroad and was a lady of great character. Never forget your history as it is an excellent history of the world.

Chapter 6
Giving Back

The importance of giving back is a critically essential for black men who have made it in our society. The young black men and boys need you in your community. You should develop a plan to attack your community. An idea I would suggest which is simple is to identify an elementary school in a black neighborhood or a private school network with the teacher and mentor a young man. Read to them about black history and show them how to balance time.

My father always told me to teach a man to fish he will always know how to feed himself. I agree with my father. My philosophy is to also teach them our history and how to excel and navigate in this world, and they will always see the way. They need to know how to put on a tie. The young men need to speak correctly and professionally. A firm handshake also goes a long way. Start with one young man and help him find his way until he can fly on his own. Be a father figure for this young man, if needed. Ladies, there is nothing wrong with contacting good organizations about your child to get a tutor or mentor for your child.

Many non-profit organizations can help and give back to your child. There are sports teams as well that give back to the community. The importance of giving back is vital for us as African Americans. There are many of us who live in plush homes and drive nice cars. We owe it to our ancestors to help pull someone else up. We must sacrifice our time and resources. We must figure out as men who are successful how you can give back to the young, underprivileged around us. There were many that paved the way and died for us to sit and relax and watch sports. We can give one day or spend time coaching sports in order to teach kids about the important values in life.

Give of yourself after your job. Your sacrifice to help a young African American boy grow into a responsible and achieving man will bring you great mental reward. An African American child must see a figure of someone who looks strong and healthy like them. We must show positive imaging versus rapping street hustling because it does not get you anywhere but prison or an early grave. Many rappers do not last long these days. There are a few who have longevity. Jay-Z is one of them. When you look at rappers or community activists such as Tupac and Stanley Tookie Williams, founder of the Crips, they are no longer with us. The businessmen such as Kenneth Chenault, Barry

Gordy, Earl C. Graves, P-Diddy, and Michael Jordan all have highly successful careers. These are images we must aspire to.

The importance of giving back is a sense of pride, courage, and integrity. When you give back to a cause, person, or place, it shapes who you are and helps change your perspective on your own life. Giving back has been an active reason why many African Americans have persevered. Churches and community organizations and leaders have paved the way for others. There are figures like Frederick Douglass who sacrificed his life with his voice body, mind, and soul to ensure his people had a voice in this society. He fought with the abolitionists to ensure African Americans were freed and were able to compete in the country their ancestors built. Individuals like Madam C.J. Walker created jobs for hundreds of African Americans with the money she acquired from selling her hair products. She made sure it got back to her community.

When you give back, you are laying a foundation for another to walk and enjoy based on the sacrifice you made. Individuals gave back to help others and it was a way of showing they had not forgotten their historical roots. The importance of what I was taught in giving back is you want to leave this world better than when we lived in it. As at the beginning of American history, we had African Americans fighting hard so there would be no more slavery and lynchings. So as when Dr. King was alive black folks in the 1960's were fighting and sacrificing for us to have the right to vote and live a better life.

These individuals did not waste time. They wrote and sacrificed. They were dignified in their perspective to have a plan to help those who clearly had been neglected. These individual are different in their approach, especially when we see what is happening today. These people believed in collectively giving back to heritage. They were not individualistic as some are once they reach a certain plateau. They are not of the mindset that they cannot give back to the community from whence they have come.

Individuals like Maynard Jackson and Andrew Young fought for the African Americans in Atlanta to have a city they could benefit from and help make it what it is today. It was imperative so it was not lost in the terrible times of the early 1980's. These men could have focused solely on themselves and would have lived well but they believed in sacrifice and giving back. Men like Thurgood Marshall, who became the Supreme Court Justice made sure his presence had a positive impact on the justice system for people of color. He wanted the law to be fair for African Americans during his time on the earth. His sacrifice not only made it better for us when he served but it continues to impact us right now as you are reading this book. We must require of ourselves to give back for a more positive future for our kids and our own lives.

If you are an attorney looking out on the city in which you work, give back to the local urban high-school. They could use a mentor like you. If you are an African American, you owe your people. One day is better than no day. Talk about the experiences you have been through. If you are the only African American in your company, mentor others. Otherwise, all of your work may be lost or all your work will be lost and your legacy will be diminished. Be an excellent example for young African Americans behind you.

As a college graduate, you may also find mentor opportunities at your alma mater. There is an opportunity to call the institution you attended and express your interest in mentoring a black student. Try to fit it into your schedule once a month. It is essential to pass on your knowledge of how you attained your position. Having an engaging one on one conversation is necessary. It is essential to give these young people tools to live and do better. They might be the business owners to hire your children one day. Please take the time to help your people.

In athletics, men like Muhammad Ali, Curt Flood, and Jackie Robinson sacrificed to point out injustices in sports and help others. In

46

sports today, athletes do not realize the pain and suffering many of the past and present endure. Many (not all) millionaire athletes are paid an enormous amount of money and live like kings but these athletes don't realize how important it is to give back. When resources are not an object, you can give back by building parks and stadiums and schools in the urban communities. Men like Curt Flood challenged the major league baseball trade clause. Through his initial efforts, many major league players benefit from his sacrifice. Curt would go back to the community where he grew up in Oakland. Men like Jim Brown showed the NFL that he could control his destiny. Jim Brown used his NFL money and notoriety to stand up for issues in the black community as far as helping young black men stay out of prison and gangs. Torii Hunter is a former baseball player and he helped build a stadium for the University of Arkansas at Pine Bluff and he didn't even attend there for college. There are many ways to make a positive impact.

As successful black men, we owe it to our communities and organizations to reach back and help train young men who look like us. Train them on the path they may face in their lives. It is crucial to be mentors to our black boys and brothers to carry our legacies and history for success in our lives. Giving back is more fulfilling than material

47

items. Plant the seeds today for an even more powerful existence of

young black men tomorrow.

Chapter 7
Readers are Leaders

As a young man, my mother and father had me reading quite often and going to the library. My mother would bring books home from the book-mobile. I would sit in my room and read. My joy of reading has taken me around the world through books. I have become a stronger person through reading. My mother also set it up in my room so I had a library and plenty of books to read at my disposal.

Young African American boys need books to read. Take them to the library at their school or a local public library. Make time to take your child to learn. Challenge them to read books about black history, world history, and finances. Get your children accustomed to reading the daily news headlines or current affairs. All of this can be found on a smartphone or laptop. As a parent, it would be excellent to have a bookshelf in your house. You would like your children to know that you have a vast interest in reading as well. These days, however, reading on devices is becoming more and more common.

In America, many studies are always trying to portray the image that African Americans do not read. The myth can be dispelled with you. You can be influential in creating a child who can read, analyze, and be more creative. Black boys should have knowledge of Dr. George Washington Carver, Dr. Charles Drew, and others alike. Reading the bible and having a foundation in Christ will also keep them morally grounded. Put pictures of positive black figures around their rooms. We often become what we see. Reading positive affirmations and books on successful individuals can help shape their minds. This will hopefully ward off selling drugs and the dangerous lifestyles glorified in some urban communities. Discuss alcoholism and the effects of excessive alcohol usage and drug addiction with your children. These are real epidemics in our communities.

Have your child read history about black colleges and the significant figures that attended those great institutions. Read to your children if they are very young. Read to them about great men like Dr. Martin Luther King Jr. and Malcolm X. Malcolm X was self-educated while in prison. Read to them about the history of Egypt and the great Hannibal, a mighty African general. Cultivating their young minds is essential. Read about the history of slavery. Discuss the significance of women like Sojourner Truth and how she was one of the best orators of her time. Books about Harriet Tubman and her success give inspiration to young minds. Read about the greats like Madam C.J. Walker who revolutionized hair care for African Americans and provided numerous jobs for our community.

The person with knowledge has the power to influence many lives. God has given us the talent and ability to use our brains with analytical skills and rational thoughts. Reading is a fundamental exercise in which you gain knowledge, confidence, and awareness. No one can take it from you. When children read, they visualize and their views change. It is good to take a child outside of their comfort zone into a world of greater possibilities.

It is an important aspect as well as to take away video games and start implementing reading as an essential key component to imagery. Imagery is everything in our society. It is the way we are shaped to interact and survive. Many of our young people need to know of possibilities beyond their local confinements and communities.

Get information about black colleges and global financial possibilities. The news weeks of the world educate journal publications and sports magazines. The small steps of reading can and will save lives in a world where young black men are dying more and more. Black men are also neglected of opportunities to succeed in life. We must create opportunities and not wait for someone to give them to us.

Reading can cultivate fresh ideas of success and chances for survival in a jungle of many traps against a young African American.

Focusing on investing and giving your child access to information to help positively shape their minds is key. A simple tablet or physical library is worth the cost and effort to build and cultivate your young child. Focus on the aspect that you will invest in the future for this young life. Go to the flea markets and buy books at local bookstores or go on the internet. There are plenty discounted books at our disposal. The importance is to have your child read from a young age in order to give their lives a boost or the inspiration needed. Create an opportunity for your child to survive and thrive and be good, strong black men.

Chapter 8
Legacy Awakening

Young or old, we must not ever forget our past. Those family or community members who sacrificed and perhaps died for you to live, vote, and become educated are to be acknowledged. We owe it to ourselves to be respectful human beings. In this life as an African American, there is no reason for you to be ashamed. Look at the significant achievements around you. Many African Americans are doing amazing things. We had our first black president. Look at our history. Many slaves taught themselves to read and then lead our people. We have been leaders since we graced the soil of America.

Crispus Attucks is a patriot who died in the revolutionary war. In our illustrious history, we had an all-black army which was the 54th Massachusetts. They fought valiantly in the civil war. Search deep the black fraternities of men of courage who belong to Kappa Alpha Psi, Alpha Phi Alpha, Omega Psi Phi, Phi Beta Sigma, and Iota Phi Theta. Their legacies are profound. They are not a part of a gang or a lazy culture. They are a part of a brotherhood. Often times, the media overlooks the positive images happening in our communities or the positive feats these brothers conquer. They highlight harmful images portraying a culture of generations of senseless violence from California to the New York.

You have to understand your history in order to become the very best you can be. Have good character. Be on time. Have integrity. Never give anyone a chance to destroy your character. You are intelligent and beautiful. Love God and respect your ancestors. Join organizations or be around like-minded as you. The Urban League, NAACP, local youth non-profits give your life so others can make it. Awaken your greatness!

Read, learn, start a business, and thrive. Forgive those who speak negatively against you. Dress well, eat healthy, workout often. Never be afraid of success. Be humble enough to ask for help. Remember the warriors in front of you who paved the way for you. If they could make it, we can as well. We have nothing to fear. The Bible says, "If God is for you, who can be against you?" Have faith in God.

Leave your legacy strong. As Africans Americans, we have lost friends and family members to gun violence, sickness, and disease. Some of the gun violence we have experienced, unfortunately, is due to one black person killing another black person. You must awaken your greatness and leave your legacy for others to admire. Create a heritage

that cannot be denied or erased from history.

Chapter 9
Don't be Discouraged

In this life, we have had many struggles. Some may continue to occur every day or at least seem that way. I remember being a youth in third grade. I was not organized and that seemed okay since I was just a kid learning how to live. My 3rd grade teacher was Mrs. Mazui. She asked me to get a book. I never got the book because I could not find it. When Mrs. Mazui learned that I didn't have the book, she picked up my desk and threw it over in front of all the other classmates. I was devastated. I did not understand the rationale nor did I know how to process the experience. So, I cried. I knew at that moment that life was not fair.

I told my mom and dad but they did nothing. There was no parent/teacher conference. At that moment, I had to make a choice. I told myself this would not defy me or define me. I was determined to make it and prove she could not control my destiny. I went on to graduate from high school and college.

I have another vivid memory from childhood. I was five years old playing summer baseball for the Oakland Parks and Recreation Joe Morgan T-shirt league. I was up to bat. I hit a screaming shot to right field in the green ivy. As I was running to first base, the first baseman tripped me. I pushed him and started crying. My dad and all the kids were laughing. I recall it being a muddy day. Something in me knew I needed to keep running and I had a split second decision to make. Turns out, it was a home run. My feelings were deeply hurt. That taught me that in life, we must continue to push forward, even in the face of disappointment.

At age 14, my coach told me that I would not be picked for the Oakland Babe Ruth All-Star team. The coach called me and said, "Son, we will have to let you go." I cried all night. I was mortified. I told my dad I was better than all the other players. I truly believed I was the best. I told my dad I was going back and make the All-Star team the next year. I started my quest the next day. I took one hundred balls at every practice. I worked hard. I made to not one All-Star team but two the following year. I was the representative for the Oakland Babe Ruth team as well as a private team called Oakland Select. The Oakland Babe Ruth team played in El Segundo, CA. The Oakland Select team played in Edmonton, Canada. It is so amazing how things can turn around in just one year.

About nine years later, I was coaching with my dad. We coached the Kappa youth baseball team and the coach who cut me from all-star team saw me. He came up to me and apologized for everything that happened when I was playing on his team. He said I should have been on the team. The coach acknowledged to me he was proud that I came back to the coaching to play the following year and proud to see me coaching in the area.

There was a time when my ex-father in law put me down. He was living with me at the time. I was looking for a job while I was attending a school around the corner from me in Berkeley, CA. He was talking loud to my ex-wife and said, "You know your cousin got a job with the Berkeley Fire Department." I got fired up and told myself I was going to get a good job quickly. Within a week I got a job working as a chauffeur. The position trained me two days and sent me out on the third day in San Francisco.

I was doing okay at first and a problem arose. I had a ride to California hospital. Sadly, I did not have my GPS and this was during the time when my phone did not have GPS either. It is always important to be well prepared for work the night before. I could not read my printed map directions. So I called the dispatch and got directions. I could tell that the customer was a little upset with my question. I asked the customer to please calm down. I will get you to your proper destination. He started screaming and told me he has never had this happen before. I explained to him that it was my first day. I got him to his destination and he seemed fine.

The next day I was fired because the owner said I did not know my way around San Francisco. He said he made a mistake hiring me and his dispatcher did not like me. I told him, "Sir, please. I need this job." I had just moved and I need this income. He tells me to get my check and get out. I was trembling inside with anger. I told him I was capable of driving in San Francisco. I explained that I'm college educated and I help kids and do all kinds of things. I said, "God will show you. I can do this job." I walked away and continued to look for employment. Two days later, I was offered a job working at Bow Tie Transportation. I started working in June of 2011. I was the first runner-up for Rookie of the Year. This job also required me to drive to San Francisco every day and I did it successfully.

The point here is that I have encountered people throughout life telling me things I could not do. The key is that I had confidence in my God and in myself. That kept me going. I had courage and tenacity. Instead of giving up, I allowed these people to motivate me. I am doing better than ever.

Sanders Strickland, a neighbor down the street from where I grew up in Oakland told me, "A good man is like a beach ball in a pool.

59

You can't hold him down." All I am saying is we must continue to rise to greatness even in the face of obstacles and adversity.

In the spring of 2010, I met one of the leaders from Berkeley Youth Experiences. Her name was Ms. Roberts and I met her at the HBCU forum. She expressed a need for volunteers at the youth facility. I took her up on it and started to volunteer my time. This was 5 years after returning home with my bachelor's degree. I had a fascinating start with this company. I had come back home excited to make a change in Oakland. My goal was to help the young black men who are all around East Oakland and West Oakland. During this time, there was still a lot of senseless violence. People were being killed over drugs, women, and turf they did not own.

I was listening to a local urban radio station and they announced a black college expo. I called the director and got a booth. Then, I called Saint Augustine's, my alma mater, and they sent me some materials to help me get started. My dad and I hustled to set up a booth and I began recruiting kids from all over the Bay Area to attend Saint Augustine's. I was invited to come and speak to a group of kids by a counselor from the center.

I would bring black college recruiters with me and my mentor, Harold Logwood. He was a member of Phi Beta Sigma fraternity and also a graduate of Howard University. Marvin Clark is a recruiter for Langston University. We would inspire the youth to look at college as an option instead of the streets. We did our best to motivate the kids.

I would bring in my fraternity brothers of Kappa Alpha Psi, who were successful in real estate and business. One brother was George Hill and another was Craig Long. I extended myself to others in the community. There was a brother who provided insight on HBCU survival tactics. We will never know the true impact of helping these young men but we know our influence helped save some men in Oakland.

There was a time I brought in a movie called Tales from the Hood for the young men to watch. There is a scene where a gang member played by comedian, Joe Torry, is shot and killed by another gang member. Well, he is sent to a mind deprivation center. He is given a choice to live. The doctor puts him on a table and he starts spinning and seeing images of black men being killed by being hung in trees. There were more black men shooting each other and powerful images of violence. The doctor tells him he can turn away from the violence and live or continue down the path and die. He chose his track and he woke up with the gang members over him. They killed him. One young man got up out of their seats on that particular scene. This scared many of them. It was important to show this film because these young men needed a scared straight program. I wanted to show them that the gang banging leads to something more detrimental.

I started to attend a church called Berkeley Mt. Zion. The church was in the same vicinity of the Berkeley Youth Facility. One particular Sunday, I was leaving the church and I ran into the director of the Berkeley Youth facilities. He asked me if I was looking for a job. I told him, "yes." He said okay and asked me to call him Monday.

I called him on that Monday. I was interviewed and got the job two weeks later. My first office mate was Alexis. She was very nice but at times apprehensive about training me as a caseworker and providing clarity about the role. I'm not sure if that was her role but she was given the assignment. It's like that sometimes with non-profit businesses. About a month into the job I learned to stand on my own. I figured out the job functions. Shortly after I started to get the hang of the position, I received an e-mail from my church member who hired me asking me to come to his office. I went into his office and he told me he was moving me to a different workspace in order to make things more accommodating for my office mate. I didn't think he was being completely truthful with me at the time.

As it turns out, my office mate wanted me out of the office suite so she could move her friend girl in there with her. Instead of being upfront about her desire to have her friend in there, she made up something to tell the manager about how we were not getting along. This was clearly not true. I moved to a new office and I thought it would be a fresh start. It turned out to be a workplace disaster as my old office mate tried to have vacuum the room every other week. She was verbally rude to me. I prayed not to go off her on have because I was trying to hold onto a job and I was not even off probation.

In my mind, we should want to help elevate each other professionally. We are not here to hurt one another. Before getting hired at the facility, I helped as many young African American kids I could, given the resources. For this co-worker to have the audacity to try to taint my credibility was shameless and distasteful.

I would think back on my upbringing. I watched my grandmother run her own hair salon business in Berkeley, CA. My mother always had me involved in the school district's annual Oratorical Fest. I always gave speeches from famous historical black leaders. These experiences led me to understand helping people would be a critical part of my life. I hope people reading this book understand your respective history as it helps shape who you are and who you will become.

As our young men and women look at our prison systems, I hope they come to the conclusion that it is not a place they ever want to be. Many of our men and women are there and at such high rates. The systems in place to make this the reality is disheartening. Therefore, I'm proud of any black man who is not in the system. That man is a leader and defying the odds of societal traps set up for their failure.

I once created a collage of black achievers. Men and women leaving examples of how to dress appropriately; many are celebrities or entrepreneurs. I wanted to show the young people why pulling up your pants and dressing the part is essential. I would display a positive image of a man being respectful and let the youngsters see it. I wanted to demonstrate what I learned.

The fraternity my dad and I are a part of started in Bloomington, Indiana on January 5, 1911, by ten men who wanted to be a beacon of light for other young black men. They wanted these men to be better and focus on God.

There was one particular time when I brought in a movie called, "Bring Your "A" Game" directed by Mario Van Peebles. It was geared towards helping young men. The documentary discusses the pitfalls many young African America boys face. The movie examines the pitfalls many young black men fall into, such as drugs and violence, and how to avoid those pitfalls. It shows how most young boys growing up think they only have two choices, entertainment or athletics. This is not true but this is their perception based on their environments.

Chapter 10
Moments of Encounter

One morning, about six years ago, I left my house in El Sobrante, California about 2:35 in the morning. On my journey, I thought long and hard about all the potential issues I could encounter. There are many deer that could cross the road at any time. I was headed to work. Since I had to be out of the house so early and I stayed in a wooded area at the time, it was important to be extra careful.

In addition to the animals and potential drunk driver, there was always a possibility of a speed trap. This poses issues another set of issues. There are several threats of being profiled by cops in the neighboring city. They were more like security detail, in my opinion. Then, there was the state of California Highway Patrol. I occasionally drove about 5 mph over the speed limit just to cut down on some time.

During this season in my life, I was dealing with extreme stress. My father had a stroke. There was a lot going on with the family and I didn't need anything additional to add to it. This particular morning, I was a little behind schedule. As a result, I was speeding around a city called Walnut Creek in California. I was trying to make up about 4 minutes in my commute. I hated being late and I just never knew what side of the bed the dispatcher (at my job) woke up on that day. He never seemed to understand any type of grace period for tardiness. All this being the case, I decided to push it right around this exit in Dublin, California.

I must admit, I made my Honda CRV look like a Porsche. All of a sudden, my stomach dropped and the hair on the back of my head starts to stand up. I see the California Highway Patrol officer speeding up on me. I realized at that moment that I messed up by speeding and this was all my fault. I could have given myself ten minutes had I been disciplined enough to get out of the house on time. The cop is on the bullhorn and tells me to get off the next freeway exit. I complied and pulled into a Bank of America parking lot. The cop pulls up to me and says I would like to see your license and registration.

Rule number one for any young or old black man is to always have a license and registration ready for the cops out the window when they approach your vehicle. The cop then tells me to get out of the car. I complied. He then proceeds to try to give me a sobriety test. This was unnecessary as I was not impaired. I was just on my way to work. He proceeds and tells me to follow his finger and tell him what direction. I complied. He proceeds to tell me that my car smells like weed. I told him that if I smoked weed, I would not do it in the morning. At this point, I responded to him arrogantly. I don't advise young people to do at all in this day and age as it could get you killed instantly. I was fed up at this point. The truth of the matter is that I didn't even smoke weed so he was making an assumption that didn't even apply to me. By this time, I'm still complying with everything but I was a bit shocked and now nervous. I put my hands back in my pockets and the officer yells at me and tells me to take them out and follow directions. His partner tells me I can go sit down in my car. I did what the officer instructed. A few minutes later, the officer handed me a ticket, for speeding. Sadly, this was four days before Christmas.

The following March, I went to court in Walnut Creek, California. The goal was to try to get the ticket lessened from 489 dollars. The night before my hearing, I was discussing the ticket with my ex-wife and the possibility of getting a judge who would empathize with my situation. Unfortunately, this did not happen. In fact, the presiding judge seemed to already have a preconceived notion of how he was going to rule against me before I pleaded my case. Here's how it went down. In this particular courtroom, you had to stand in line. While waiting my turn, I witnessed several cases. It made me realize how much the double standards still exist. There was one case in particular that caught my attention. A young Caucasian kid was there for speeding just like me. He asked for mercy and the judge decided to give him traffic

68

school to keep points off his license. Witnessing that case, I was almost certain I had a high probability of getting the same treatment. As I got to the front of the courtroom, I pleaded my case. I too asked for mercy. I explained that I was sorry. I told him I'm a responsible man who has a master's degree and had just made a poor decision by speeding. I also explained that having points on my record would adversely impact my livelihood because I was a chauffeur. The reason I was speeding was that I was trying to prevent a negative mark against me by the dispatcher at my job. As a result, I made a poor judgment to speed and was caught by a California Highway Patrolman. I went on to explain that while I was able to keep my job, I lost time and money dealing with this situation. It is important to make wise decisions and have good time management skills. Because of this and what I witnessed earlier in the courtroom, I instantly plead "no contest." I was thinking to myself the judge would give me the same sentence he gave the young man earlier. I was wrong. Instead, he told me in a very harsh manner, "Give me your license; it is suspended." Needless to say, I was shocked and distraught. I had my license suspended for thirty days.

I had to make a judgment ask our lord for protection. I went home driving very cautiously. I was hurt because the judge was not more understanding, especially, since I had been an upstanding citizen.

I suggest anyone who gets a ticket ask questions at the courthouse. Observe the difference in how the judge treats people based on race. I learned to drive with caution and prepare and not be in a rush to work. To make matters worse, a few days later I heard another story related to being pulled over by the cops. A friend of a friend was pulled over. She was driving to work going 93 mph in a 65 mph zone. The cop who pulled her over did not give her a ticket but a warning instead. He told her not to go over the speed limit more than ten miles per hour and to drive safely. She is Caucasian. There is the double standard staring me in the face once again.

So, make smart moves and cover yourself well. I learned that God will protect and guide me in all situations. He will cause the worse things to work out favorable if I trust Him, seek Him, and put Him first. Well, as much as I hate to admit it, I had the grace of God with me for the next 30 days. I drove the next 30 days because that was the only way to feed my family. Thankfully, I was not pulled over or profiled. I drove very cautiously. My license was reinstated just after the 30 days ended.

I am an example of someone who has endured many tests but still has a strong and focused mind. You must be an eagle and chameleon to make it in this world. I have to thank God for keeping me during these difficult seasons in life. My goal is to learn from the bad decisions, make better ones, and inspire others so hopefully, they won't make the same bad choices I've made. I continue to carry the torch and never give up.

Chapter 11
Making Smart Choices

As young African American men, many face rising cases of homicides. This stems from self-hatred taught during slavery and drugs that were brought into our communities by the government. This was by design to harm and to kill our young men. This is also one of the reasons why our young men are in gangs and have chosen to abandon any hope for themselves.

Some of their choices come from music. Some of the rap music is harming their mentalities and the ability to approach life differently. Altering our young boys' lives and persuade them to think money, sleeping with women, and drinking is the most positive things they can do in life. In some communities, our young people play video games that can teach violence and aggression. Playing violent video games can alter your mind because it desensitizes you to violence. Our young men must make wiser choices about what they allow to come into their psyche.

We have many situations of drugs and homicide in our community that affect us. Just because you are a product of that particular environment does not mean you must continue to perpetuate the plague of sickness that has claimed the lives of many of our young and old. We must cultivate a mind of better choices and realize that drugs and quick money are not lasting.

In reality, drug dealers do not live long on the streets. They either die trying to protect their turf or end up in prison. As a community, we must individually take it on our shoulders to think of methods and ways to become successful in this life. There are many other choices besides killing one another over rage. We have an obligation to learn our history even if it means going to the library, listening to audiobooks, or watching YouTube. There is information at our fingertips about jobs and other things we can do to survive in this world. The choice is ours to leave one situation and go to something that helps us grow and become better.

As a community, we can think outside the box when we want to survive in a system that wants to keep us closed minded. We must be willing to explore other places in life beyond the neighborhood in which we were born and raised. If you live in Oakland, for example, try traveling to Sacramento or San Francisco or San Jose to have a different cultural perspective. We must choose between traveling and seeing other things outside of our community. Make choices to go to the local bookstore, locate African American authors, and read.

We must make it a priority to understand what is going on in the world in which we live. Young people must realize they do not have to be a thug. It is okay to go to local churches that teach about how to enhance your life. Mentors can talk to these young people and help them get them out of their situations. Bring them a book to read that will enlighten them.

Some argue that rapping and being a thug is all the young people may know. I would like to challenge that and say show them another life. There are black doctors, lawyers, scientists, professors, and pastors, to name a few. These images can be found easily. Challenge the young people to find out about these people. They can make a vision board. The young people may need help in the way of creativity and new ideas in order to be exposed to things out of their norm. If you are an athlete playing for a division one team at a well-known university, stay focused on the sport you are playing. It is easy to get distracted and get off course. As an athlete from an urban area, it is important to build a network of support with other minority athletes and student organizations for emotional and educational support.

Stay away from drugs, alcohol, shoplifting, or anything that could have you put in jail or expelled from school. The right choices on those campuses are critical for your survival there and your life after

74

college. Those colleges are different worlds from the urban setting where you may have grown up. As you consider your college choices, make sure you consider all aspects of the environment of the school you plan to pursue.

I would suggest looking into black college football or a program that wants to see you graduate. At a black college, you have a better chance of graduation than at some of the more well-known colleges. Make the choice to get a degree. A football career can end abruptly due to unforeseen circumstances such as injuries or competition. Our choices to survive are critical for the integrity of our families and the legacy we will leave behind. It is important to be good fathers and live to be grandfathers. Men must make choices to live right and stay strong.

Just because the clubs are open does not mean we have to go all the time. Calculate your steps and relax. Think about the things you want to do. We must stop reacting and think things through to make the best decisions. Think about your life as a ship and think about how you want to plan safe trips to each destination without destroying the vessel. Become the master of your destiny and the captain of your ship. Be an eagle and sour to new places instead of with the pigeons always with the big groups. Stop talking about how happy you are doing the same things over and over and venture out. Be different and make winning choices in your life. Be truly happy and strong in your life. Stand strong on your voyage.

Choose to marry a good woman and treat her like a queen. Choose to be a doctor or whatever you feel that can help someone. Life is a blessing when you can help someone reach another level of success. Choose to respect others and defend yourself when you need to. Love your brothers like yourself. Love God. Value life. Live strong. Enjoy being alive and strive to be a part of African American history in a positive way. Be a leader and an intelligent leader in your community.

Left to Right: Me, Marshane, NBA Hall of Famer Bill Russell, Willie, and Alex (son of Bob Maynard)

Kappa Baseball Program – Day with the Oakland Athletics and Hall of Fame MLB Joe Morgan

I'm encouraging the team after a championship loss

Team photo after the championship game

Grambling State University 2008 Graduate

Chapter 12
The News

When watching the news, we must understand that the news is designed to sell many advertisements during only about a fourteen-minute news segment. It is important to look at the headlines when they involve a story about a young or old black man. We almost always hear young African Americans shot and killed over a drug-related crime gone wrong. At the beginning of the news segment, you might hear there are reports of young black men robbing people in a certain section of town.

Studies have shown time and time again that when you hear and see images of crimes involving blacks, they often do an injustice to the race and show people in the worse light. These television programs know exactly what they are doing. African American men are not the only people who have been violent in the communities in which we live. The news programs cast black men as violent, scary human beings.

When you heard about the hurricane Katrina situation in New Orleans, you heard about young black men looting and raping young women. Instantly, when you think about those images, anarchy comes to mind. The same news reporters would say that a Caucasian man was finding food for survival. The way the video footage of both images is portrayed, you would think it is a different story. In reality, it is the same.

If a Caucasian child is murdered, the news always follows up on stories until the killer is found. The majority of murders of black children go unresolved and fall off the radar right after they occur. This is the norm, so we have become immune to it in our society. This should not ever be condoned.

In no way is killing anyone right. Every news station in the country is the gatekeeper of public perception. They impact the way people think about their communities. The news stations should be informational centers for our community with information on how to stop specific plagues. The news stations could report on positive stories in the community. Civic organizations and mentors go into the communities and help the disadvantaged youth.

When watching the news in your particular area of the country, listen and be cautious about what's there what they are broadcasting most frequently. If broadcasters are continually talking about black people in a negative light, you may need to limit your intake. I remember the issue regarding Barry Bonds, a former professional baseball player, who was accused of using some illegal enhancement substance. This was in the news almost every day. Start to question why particular stations have an objective that could be misguided and not ethical on purpose. Stations have intentions to distort images of reality. So if you are watching a television news broadcast over and over and they play the same imagery for over twenty years, there is a problem. People tend to get programmed by that type of news.

One must think deeply when you see images on sports programs that depict us as drug dealers un-worthy of college scholarships and money in professional sports. There is a problem with the imagery that has been created by these television networks. We must report our own news by getting a camera and reporting the truth in your particular community. Technology like YouTube and Periscope is making this more feasible. Put it on the internet or on your website. Find solutions as to why there is black on black violence in your community. We know we are intelligent and working hard every day to make a living in our communities.

Don't believe the hype of what these networks are trying to portray. We must understand that these images are not true about the majority of African Americans. We are inventors, entrepreneurs, pharmacists, and politicians. We are not the negative images that are

81

portrayed in most media outlets. We must understand reporters are only human and most network owners don't look like us. They cannot define you. No one can but you.

Most newsrooms are run by Caucasian perspectives of reality. When viewing people as African Americans in a negative light, how can they engage the news from a balanced perspective? There are some news directors who don't care what African Americans have done positively, in my opinion. If they did, civic organizations would have more air time. The news media would host town hall meetings. If the news media changed its strategies regarding the way they report the news, perspectives would change. Some people do not get any other perspective outside of the one they see on television. Be keen and intellectual while forming decisions based on what you see and hear on the news. Listen for false narratives and consider other sources of information.

In the black community, we have many achievements. Until the news stations start airing positive stores about African American people, we will continuously be viewed negatively by other citizens in our community. The news is a powerful tool and can be very dangerous. Always be aware of the deceptive images because you are a king, a prince, a business leader, a civic leader, and all the greatest positions are yours in this world. Believe when you look in the mirror you are beautiful and intelligent being. You are not what someone else says you are; God has designed you for greatness. Black men soar to the top of the highest mountains. You are eagles.

Chapter 13
Treat Her Like a Lady

A lady is a queen. The mother of your child is vital to your child's development and nurturing. We must as black men appreciate our strong, intelligent queens. These women are often focused and love us. As black men, we owe it to these women to be considerate, strong, and independent brothers. We must treat our women with the same respect we would give our mothers.

In thinking about your mother, we must consider our mother as a queen. She spent nine months carrying you. Honor women by building and growing with them. Think about the most precious jewel in the world. That is your lady. She is not a sex object; she is a beautiful specimen down to her core. Love this woman who gives her heart. A queen will sacrifice with you all the way to the end.

As men, we must not verbally abuse our women. We must be there and support her and trust her. We should want to meet at a common ground and succeed together. Young brothers should get to know a lady. When she talks about dreams, help her achieve them. When working as a team, you can get the best results. You can get much better results than if you just focused on doing things by yourself.

84

As a black man, we must learn from our ladies. Many of them are strong in lots of different ways. When you take her out, treat her. Older, more established gentlemen bring flowers every week or something thoughtful she can use or enjoy. Spend time with her family. You must be respectful and look her parents in the eyes. It's important to have a firm handshake. If you treat her like she is the most precious lady on this earth, her parents and other family members will be able to tell right away.

When you are in a relationship, be faithful. When men cheat, they poison the relationship. No man is perfect but pray and always be aware of distractions. You must make wise choices. Be the man she has never seen before. Keep God first in your relationship. Pray often. Pray together. Appreciate the time and resources God has afforded you. You are blessed with time to enjoy with your partner. Plan things together. Make thing enjoyable and do things for the enrichment of your lives. Take a class together. Enjoy concerts, book signings, church revivals, traveling, and the list goes on. Also, go to relationship therapy classes so you can better understand one another if you are planning to get married.

Never degrade your lady or speak harshly to her. She must be adored. Never allow money fights to become an issue in your relationship. You should work as hard as you can to be the best provider you can be. Attend church regularly. It is important to have faith in God. Travel to different places. Take pictures and build memories to cherish. Set goals together and hold each other accountable. Then, the goals can be achieved. Stay focused and your goals can be accomplished.

Educate each other. Learning should never cease to exist in the relationship. It must be a continuing experience. African American men are willing to listen to your woman. Understand her thoughts and perceptions about matters in life. She has a lot to offer you in your life. As men, we should work with our women to make sure that their lives are peaceful and structured. Protect your queens from harm and enjoy her mind, body, and soul.

Women are our lifelines and continue our beautiful people growing strong. Treat your women right in your heart and you cannot go wrong. A true queen only wants what is best for you. Keep her protected with love, care, and spiritual guidance to see her preserved for years to come.

Chapter 14
Raising Champions

In today's society, African American boys must be nurtured with closer attention than any other people in our society. The images across the nation are heart-shattering. Young African American boys are going to jail at younger ages. Young boys are being labeled with attention deficit disorders in their local schools. These boys are suspended for showing up to class one minute late or even saying something in class the teacher deems threating. In some cases, the teachers pick on these boys for anything. The climate is clear and dangerous for our young African American boys who attend schools in underfunded areas.

The recipe for success is up to the parents. There has to be a plan for the child's overall success. Let's take a look at a few survival tactics for boys in the 21st century. Try to get him engaged in math and science at a young age. Put your child in advanced schools and be a very involved parent in your child's educational life. It is very critical to make sure that you teach your child African American history so they cannot be deterred by the miseducation that many of these schools around our country. There is a distorted view of history being taught in schools today. Educators continuously lie about history and who we are as a great people.

We must build that history back as parents. Train your child and guide them in the direction of your desired plan. Have images of successful African Americans with a vision board. As the old saying goes, "Image is everything."

Have a slogan on the wall with motivational praise. Tell your children they are smart and beautiful. Take time on Saturdays to help your child explore. Get them involved in sports, travel outside of your community, and see something a little different.

Monitor the television. This is important. Buy books for your child. Visit the local library and get inspirational authors for your child from an infant all the way up to high schools. Have them interested in sports, science, debate team sports so that may learn how to work with others and build self-esteem. Show images of strong black inventors, black mayors, and other successful people in their world. It makes a lasting impression on a child when they know more than being a rapper or athlete in life.

Children have to be taught how to use manners and be polite. It is still okay to be kind. This can be done without losing their creativity. Being aware of their surroundings is another good trait. It is important to be vigilant. As I grow older, I realize how much I didn't know about finances when I was younger. I often wonder how that happened. Is it that my parents were unaware or did I miss something along the way? It is important that children learn about finances while they are young so they don't make poor decisions as they grow older. Goal setting is also important. Goals are our destination. If we don't have them, we don't know where we are going. Basic life skills are important to a successful survival.

A young boy must understand values. Work with them and teach them to make smart choices. Not that they need to do everything right because experience is a good teacher. However, good decision making can keep them from making deadly decisions. Teach them the importance of staying away from drugs, heavy drinking, or anything that will hinder their lives. Teach them the importance of choosing friends. They need friends who are going places. Help the young men understand sex and the importance of protection when the time comes. Wearing protection can save them from the heartache of Aids and other sexually transmitted diseases. Unprotected sex can also result in getting a young lady pregnant before he is ready to be a father. Smart life choices are vitally important.

Whether the parents are homeowners or not, young people should understand real estate; the importance of owning property and managing it. Young men need to understand priorities and responsibility. They must know the difference between wants and needs. Teach them about spending habits and the fact that they don't have to buy something just because someone else has it. Additionally, some of our boys need counseling, depending on the type of environment they are in. Sometimes, they need a neutral outlet and someone to listen to them. Counseling is not a bad thing. In fact, it can be life-changing in a positive way.

Some deal with problems by being the only African American in a particular class, depending on the school district. Others want to have their fathers present. Others just need more help in school. Whatever the situation, it is perfectly fine to seek help for your son. It is important to build boys up. All young black boys need their families to help instill confidence and love, whether they know they need it or not. Sometimes, it still takes a village to raise our young black boys and to make sure they are on the path to success in this life.

The world wants our young black boys to go to prison and kill each other. We are their last hope for success. We owe them our love and support. Let's do what we can to make sure we can save them from being sucked in by this world of despair.

We are the inventors of Chicago, Fathers Dusable. We must see the potential danger for our boys and reach deep to help. We must have a plan for success. We must teach our boys that they are princes regardless of their family dynamics or even their neighborhood. Show them what hard work does and how it pays off. Keep God in their lives and stay focused on what will keep them alive and out these prisons. We are strong and intelligent people. We can change and get better with time. Our young men are the future for us. They are the future fathers and protectors many of them didn't have in their own lives. They are the pillars of our community.

Chapter 15
Tenacious Pursuit

Young African American men must be involved in their schools and motivated by pastors, coaches, teachers, community leaders, and neighbors. It is great when they are involved in leadership roles on their campuses. Young men realize at an early age that they have an important voice and we must learn how to speak up. Speak up to make a difference. Have them recite positive affirmations and quotes by national figures or community leaders. Teach them how to write letters. Some young men like to keep journals of their encounters of problems. It is important to teach them how to communicate properly with adults about issues they are encountering.

There are young men interested in being leaders in elementary school all the way up to high school. We must empower them. We must encourage them to be involved in their communities. Teach them to have pride in themselves and bring them to church. Teach them to be strong in their schools.

In high school, they must be directed toward a more positive light. The young men must learn how to be independent so they can take care of themselves. They must learn how to be generals in their own right and be a strategist to survive in a world where laser beams are aimed at their slightest mistake. Good choices must be taken very seriously for the survival of young black men.

We must promote achievement in every field of human endeavor. Our boys must learn the importance of investments. They must develop a keen sense of their surroundings and when to just walk away. Every move must be tactical. We must prepare them to make a checkmate move in this world swiftly and precisely. As the old Samurai soldiers, we must have a way in and a way out.

We must be diligent in teaching them when they see a problem in school or on their jobs, move in silence. Make observations. Once you are in a safe place, report it to the proper authorities or organization. Our young princes must be warriors and teach not to be defeated. Their minds must be strong and never focused on letting distractions take them away from their purpose of being on this earth.

The young men must love one another as brothers. Stop and listen and grow with one another in a positive way. Having fun has its place but business is serious when it comes to being effective in helping someone's life. Our young men must give back and help other young men reach a higher level of success in this culture. Be a positive part of your community. Give back like Dr. King, Malcom X, Johnnie

Cochran, Frederick Douglass, Ida B. Wells, Madam C.J. Walker, Booker T. Washington, W.E.B Dubois, Harriet Tubman, Crispus Attucks, Father Dusable, Ron Brown, Huey P. Newton, Jim Brown, Medgar Evers, Satchel Paige, Jackie Robinson, Thurgood Marshall, A. Phillip Randolph, Adam Clayton Powell, Al Sharpton, Jessie Jackson, and many other African Americans who sacrificed their time and efforts for us in this world for survival. Be a leader as many of these people were and give your money, ideas, thoughts, and time to helping life out communities. Write a book about your triumphs and sacrifices in this life. You owe them, yourself, and future generations.

Chapter 16
Art Imitating Life

In our world, your image can either help or destroy your credibility. As African American men, we are often being portrayed as thugs, drug lords, or ignorant, hyperactive, irresponsible human beings. There was a popular show entitled 'Flavor of Love' in which a 1980's rapper named Flava Flav looks like a clown and willing to have his image tarnished for a couple million dollars. We must sit and think if it's worth selling our lives and family respect for a money.

We must understand that our ancestors died in slavery for us to have the freedom to walk into a business with dignity. They did not die for us to be going to prison or feeling sorry for ourselves. They did not die so we would be killing one another or try to be a thug in your local community.

We must stop and think about the images for a second. We talk about the things we lack now or lacked in the past. We are quick to tell others we did not have anything growing up. We proclaim we will not starve even if that means resorting to selling drugs or becoming a rapper. We must understand that we are products of our communities and the images before us. If we only saw people with nice things who were dope dealers, rappers, or ball players, our minds are trained to think we must choose those things in order to have success in our own right. This is simply not the case. With the power of technology and our access to it, we are able to access so many positive images outside of the ones we see in our communities every day. We must realize what has happened to our minds.

Images were more positive and uplifting until gangster rap hit the scene in 1988 with particular gangster rap groups. Other Americans started to take a closer look at us. They were already on a mission to build more prisons. The mortuary business also started to grow during this time. The dreaded n-word was being used in many songs and there was a lot of talk about violence. We must think about the destructive images.

Let's think about the rap music of today. What do we hear? Has anything changed for the better? I hear a lot of talk about material items, gangs, drugs, and murder. Some of the music videos as well as some movies are filled with destructive images of us killing each other continuously. That is by design and on purpose whether we realize it or not. Take a step back and analyze it from a different angle.

Let's see who owns BET. While it stands for Black Entertainment Television and was previously owned by a black man by the name of Robert L. Johnson, it was sold to a company called Viacom in 2001. Some on the board of Viacom could not understand the videos and the purpose of how to live in New York, Chicago, Atlanta or Oakland or any other major inner city. They know how to make money and pay individuals but may not always understand the plight of growing up a black man in America. Many rappers in videos today brag about their possessions. A majority of the rappers rented the items displayed in these videos. It's important not to get caught up in the hype. Some rappers never lived or will ever live the life they portray. We must think critically so we are not fooled.

Take a look at yourself. Do you own a dress shirt, slacks, or any books? Let's see how many of our young black men want to be like men we see. Television promotes many famous basketball players. Some of them have many women and waste money. Others are faithful family men. Then, there are the entertainers like Jay-Z and P-Diddy who have become wealthy and are looking for more and more ways to positively impact our communities. Seeing powerful black men from diverse backgrounds can change many of our perspectives on life if we take time to look and study them. There are men like Robert Smith, a billionaire currently living in Colorado. Other men like Tyler Perry, Dr. Dre, Bishop T.D. Jakes, and Floyd Mayweather, just to name a few.

These black men are perfecting their crafts and becoming more and more influential. They are breaking barriers and busting through ceilings. There are countless other black professional men in positions of leadership and influence all across the nation but they don't get media attention. They are men with distinction and class who come from urban areas. They handle their business and still keep it real.

Imagine if we could see a show of real men who are making a real difference in our communities. This would change the narrative about black men. Some are everyday working professionals who look good in suits and have a vision beyond their own homes. They are interested in the rebuilding of Black Wall Street. I believe this will have a positive effect on our images. Often times, black men are portrayed negatively. However, we must embrace the truth about reality. The media is always focused on the negative and there are many black men doing marvelous and extraordinary things. They never make the evening news.

It is okay to talk about our trials and tribulations. Many of us have the similar stories and can help you with the destructive images. The reality of good men may not be around you every day but you must know in your heart that there are more. The television and movie executives want to control our minds. All of us. Stop, think, and realize you are not a murderer and that is not why you were created. You are beautiful, intelligent, and creative. Think of the images we see even in video games like Grand Theft Auto. Think about the basic cops and robbers games. We must understand that if we consume ourselves with video games, we start to identify with even the images there even though it is not reality. We must defeat these images and become responsible for our viewpoints. Stop embracing negative images.

Unfortunately, it is not just us who have to defeat negative images. Many in our society need to do the same. They have bought into the media's false narratives about us. That's why when we go on the train to work, many people seem afraid of us. That's because they have bought into the image that we are dangerous, abusive, thugs, and don't care about our lives. We must be more disciplined, creative, and operate in integrity.

Black men, you are not thugs. You are businessmen, family men, and leaders in your communities. Your women want you to be leaders. They are not interested in you being the thugs they see on television and in the movies. We are not alcoholics. Let's stop and think about why there are liquor stores in every black community. It's because the owners and liquor companies think we are weak, and trying to escape our reality, and we will buy it. I know you are strong and can leave it alone. Stop being deceived. Take a deep breath and let's work to change the situation. We have been caught in the maze for hundreds of years.

Change your image and change the image of your community. Influence others to do the same. Be the leader and stop following bad examples that were set before you. Go to the store and buy a tie, some shirts, and slacks. You will certainly stand out in a good way. We have the power to change our image. The power of imagery is important and we have to take advantage of it. Visualize yourself looking different. Our images are everything. When mainstream media can continue to make fools of us for money or just by exploiting our neighborhoods, it is disastrous not just for us but for the generations to come.

Many of us want success. Some of us have gained notoriety by feeding into the stereotypes because of popular movies. Many of us laughed at these movies but when that very thing hits home, we don't find it funny. It was never really a joke and at the end of the day, the joke is on you and me.

We have used the word nigga so much in speaking to each other that now people of other cultures think they can say it too. I have not and will not refer to my brothers and sisters as nigga. It's a derivative of the very negative word nigger. Our ancestors died and were referred to as niggers. People like Nat Turner, Emmit Till, and Medgar Evers, were all called niggers and now we say it in urban areas all over American like it is okay. It is not okay. In Randall Robinson's book, "Nigger," he says this word is the worst thing anyone could call another person in the English language.

Are rappers saying it like clockwork because they don't know the history? History is the reality of the present. From where we come is who we are today. If they killed Dr. King in 1968 and cried Nigger in the night sky when O.J. Simpson and Johnnie Cochran heard the words, "not guilty," then we do we continue to use this word in our own communities to speak to and reference each other.

Black men, we must take responsibility for our actions. Each one of us represents each other. College football players stay need to be more disciplined. You can't do drugs and sleep around with many women as this might harm your success. These two things have damaged many careers long after they left the college campus. The media loves it when we destroy ourselves. It is a shame too. Some colleges have stopped recruiting players from a certain region because a player has ruined the college's image. So, our actions can absolutely be a reflection of more than just the individual who did the act. It can impact the next innocent person coming behind you.

Meditate on being kind and knowledgeable. It will make you breathe a lot better when you know that life is so much better by you being your own man. Some actors look at Denzel Washington and his image. He has always been great but he has evolved over the years. Thurgood Marshall was intelligent and is still respected even after his death. On the other hand, many rappers who have been on television have long been forgotten. Dr. Martin Luther King Jr. has books and streets named after him. He was a man who had an impeccable image. He was a spiritual blessing from the Lord. Transform lives and stand for something noteworthy. Become an eagle and soar about your circumstances. You have it in you to do it. Stop being a seagull fighting over the crumbs. Young or old black men must think about what we do from every sector of the United States. We must focus on business ownership. It is important to be good fathers, sons, brothers, and uncles. Those around us are depending on us. Don't allow television, movies, and other races dictate who you are. College does not make us intelligence as Malcolm X proved. It is up to each of us to learn how to succeed in this game called life.

Take a look at your history. They did it and we can do even better. Let's continue our legacy to the top of the mountain. Rise, young warriors. Let's work together and love each other. We are all in this together no matter what shade of brown.

Chapter 17
Sports and Mentors

I loved sports as a young man. Sports made me feel strong and focused. My life in sports shaped who I am and my love of helping my people. I had a great coach when I played football for the Oakland Dynamites. His name was Coach Jackson. He was a southern man with high values and principles. He was a great mentor to me. He taught me about being a gentleman.

Coach Jackson would always speak to me and another player named D.J. about the importance of sacrifice and putting God first. He instilled the importance of being a leader in the face of adversity. He was like a father figure to me. When my parents could not pick me up, he would drive me home.

Coach Jackson died one night after dropping me off at home. He talked about life and was always happy. I will never forget his beautiful smile. He had a heart attack. I was only twelve years old at the time. When I found out he passed away, I didn't believe it. It was surreal. I was not able to say goodbye. This is why I operate with a sense of urgency. Tomorrow is not promised to any of us.

Another great coach of mine was Howard Gamble. He was my high school baseball coach when I attended Skyline High School. He had such a positive impact on my life and I will never forget him either. I remember meeting coach Gamble for the first time when he was coaching his son in the Oakland Babe Ruth League. I was much younger. Coach Gamble was a no-nonsense type of Coach when it came to baseball. In ninth grade, I was playing ball for my father for the last time in my life.

Coach Gamble had a pitching coach named Milton Owens. They would come scout me out while playing fourteen, fifteen-year-old baseball. They asked my father if I could play at Skyline for junior varsity and varsity baseball. My father told me after a game Coach Owens and Gamble wanted me to play for them at Skyline. I was ecstatic. It was an exciting time for me knowing that I would be going on to play high school baseball.

I would leave my junior high school and take the Alameda County bus up to Skyline. Coach Gamble gave me my first opportunity to play high school baseball. We made it to the championship in my freshman year. I was called upon to be a pinch runner. Unfortunately, I hesitated running to home base on a passed ball and this cost us the game at home plate. Coach Gamble was mad and the players were disappointed but we were a family and moved on from it.

I played my sophomore year as well, which would be my last season at Skyline before I transferred to Fremont high school. Coach Gamble would have our teams play all kinds of tournaments in baseball around the bay area. We were his traveling all-stars. Coach Gamble worked for the City of Oakland in janitorial services and also fixed the fields around the city of Oakland. He worked hard for Skyline baseball and loved his players. Coach made us run up this big hill called the monster and then we would come back and practice. He taught us about sacrifice and love for our teammates. He taught us the importance of giving people a chance to succeed and believe in themselves. He would, at times, drive an hour from his home in Tracy, California to Oakland two to three times a day. He made sacrifices for the players.

Coach Gamble would always take me home and pick me up on practice days. He had a green Thunderbird. He was a classy, well-dressed coach. Coach Gamble would forever be missed. He gave me a chance to succeed and believed in my baseball abilities. I thank God for him.

Coach Amin Denny, a big man with a big heart. Coach Denny went to Castlemont High School in the 1980's and went on to play football at Chico State in the early 1990's. He was my coach for one great season at Fremont High school. I left Skyline because I was a two-sport athlete and the football coach did not believe I could play varsity football at Skyline. During this time, I had a slight knee problem. I told the football coach at Skyline I could not do deep squats and his reply was that I would not play varsity at Skyline. That was a hard pill for a solid junior varsity star to swallow. I thought I was the Deion Sanders of Skyline football and baseball.

I was playing baseball the summer after my sophomore year in a World Series tournament in Las Vegas, NV. My father told me to think about what I planned to do as it relates to school going into my junior year. During my two weeks in Vegas, I played on a team called the Oakland Select in which we were all-stars who were hand-picked by a man named Alan Silver to play on the team. He was a big man for New York Life Insurance on the west coast. I went to Vegas with all of my buddies who I had known for over ten years from Oakland Babe Ruth League and Skyline. I decided that summer to transfer to Fremont. Coach Denny said he would love to have me play for him. I felt like a big draft pick. I went straight from the Oakland airport to start practicing for Fremont. That was one of the most significant moves I had made in my short life. Coach Denny had me as a third-string running back when I arrived at Fremont. I moved into the starting rotation after the second week.

My very first game was in Alameda against the Encinal Jets, not a high ranking team but well rounded. Their field was right on the water in Alameda. I ran the ball hard for Coach Denny. I was only a 5'8" and I was using my 4.5 speed to zip and zap through the holes. My running back style was patterned after Bo Jackson, Barry Sanders, Marshall Faulk, Emmitt Smith, and Russell White. I had it in my sights to be a big-time back as well.

Coach Denny had our team playing many strong teams. He believed we could play anywhere. We played schools at a high school that looked like a college. One memorable moment I remember with our team was when we traveled about four hours into the hills of Grass Valley just outside Reno, Nevada. The team we played was Nevada Union. We were pretty excited to play them as a young team from east Oakland, especially since some athletes had never been more than two hours Outside of Oakland. We were treated respectfully.

We got ready for the game. The weather was cold and ice was everywhere on the trees in this Northern California town. The stadium looked like an NFL stadium compared to what they I was used to seeing. They had about 2,000 fans. It seemed like the whole town was out at the game. As our team walked out to the field, it was getting colder and colder. Some of us were surprised about having to play in the cold. In the heat of the battle, you must be prepared for almost anything.

My mom, father, and grandmother, Jessie Sharp were all at the game supporting me. The rain started to come down hard the first play of the game. I could not believe it. We were beat bad. The only touchdowns we got were by our star player. This team beat us by twenty-one points. After the game, we all ran to get back to the bus because it was very cold and we wanted to get back to our heated rooms. Many of us caught a cold the following week.

Coach Denny taught us strength, character, and the importance of giving back to those less fortunate. He taught me to never give up. He was a man who invited the players to his house for breakfast on Saturdays just to relax and watch football. He always wanted to win and coveted the Silver Bowl Championship.

My new team played Skyline, my old team. The day of the game, it was overcast. I remember it so vividly. We wore all white Fremont Uniforms with our Tiger claws on our green helmets. We looked like the Michigan Wolverines. The Skyline Titans had their traditional red jerseys and black pants. They had an intimidating glare and their presence was felt. The friends and many of my former junior high-class mates who used to cheer me on the year before were now booing me in the stands. That was to be expected since they were loyal to Skyline. Most of them just wanted to give me a hard time. I went up for a defensive back drill and when I came down, my knee popped. I sat on the ground in pain.

Saddened that I could not play this game, it felt like the glory was mine to come back and defeat the team I played from previously. It did not happen. I cried inside when I went to the sideline to tell Coach Denny I could not go into the game. We made a glance at each other. We did not know it would be the end of a year that felt longer than two. Only God knew that cloudy day at Skyline was a blessing. I will always love Coach Denny. He is a wonderful soul who God blessed me to spend a season playing football for and I'm grateful for the opportunity. The last time I was blessed to see Coach Denny, it brought back many memories. This happened on the football field at his alma mater at Castlemont High School. His team was fighting for first place against McClymonds High School. He looked back and saw me but no words were exchanged. I miss all the other coaches who gave back with love and integrity to continue the legacy of helping young African American men like myself.

Thank you, coaches. I love you and will never forget you.

Chapter 18
Basics of Finance

A young black man must understand how to balance his budget and keep up with his finances. We cannot allow materialism to destroy the fabric of our lives. The key to financial freedom is paying you first. Put away five dollars a day or one dollar a day. Put away something. Save and invest over time and you will see a huge difference. We must understand the difference between wants and needs.

Instant gratification never got us anywhere. Quick money from drugs or get rich quick schemes are not the way to go. Patience is essential to building wealth. We must not want everything we see. Men, we must learn how to value our dollars. Calculate what will give you the most out of your dollars. Bargain shop for things you want. It will provide you with high satisfaction in knowing you saved money on an item you really wanted.

When watching an entertainer on television, please do not compare yourself to their shopping habits. Stop trying to live like people we see on television. Live below your means. Get into a credit union, a bank, or another way of taking care of your money for safe keeping. Be responsible. For any job you get, pay all bills on time and pay off debt, if you have it. Only get a credit card to establish credit. Monitor every dollar and when you buy clothes or jerseys, think about what you need before you spend your money.

Read books about money that teach you the reasoning behind what the dollar means. We must be educated on how the dollar functions. Read Dave Ramsey books and Robert Kiyosaki we must be debt free and not a borrower in life. Make smart choices about money. Black men take your time with spending money. There is money out here to be made. Stay within the parameters of the law. It is essential to make wise choices for your future and the future of those around you. You can do this and you will do it. Our black dollars can go a long way. Look at the advertisements that target black men. It is a powerful thing.

When you know your dollars are mighty, you learn how to use them more wisely. Use your ideas and your strength to make it. Use every penny to your advantage. Buy property because that is one of the keys to financial freedom. May God bless you on your journey for survival in this world.

Chapter 19
Stay Alert

In the fall of 2006, my father and I took a trip down to Louisiana to visit my eventual graduate school, Grambling State University. Having lived in Raleigh, NC before and went to college in the south already, I had an understanding of cops racially profiling young men of color. My father and I went to see the campus, meet administrators, and learn about the college. Before I get into that, I'd like to rewind back to when I was an undergraduate at Saint Augustine's College. I decided to take a trip down to the Bayou Classic with Omarion, my buddy from Oakland. We went to the game and we are lounging at a Marriott in New Orleans. We decided to head over to the Hilton to have some Coronas a short time later. We were watching the Nevada and Boise State game. As we were enjoying the atmosphere with the Grambling Alumni, a lady walked over to me. We started to talk about the game and about Grambling and she told me she was from Conyers, GA and I told her I was from Oakland. We began to talk about college and the things I wanted to do in life. She said I seemed like a very nice young man and she wanted me to meet her daughter. This was very exciting and the best news I had heard all day.

In my mind, I just knew she would be fine. She told me her daughter was Ms. Freshman at Grambling.

I told my boy Omarion and he was equally as excited for me as I was for myself. I wait for a little bit and all of a sudden this attractive young lady comes down the escalator. I am thinking to myself this is what I have been waiting for all my life. We started talking and it turned out to be a nice conversation. She told me she never met a man like me and she wanted me to attend Grambling. I told her I wanted to attend for grad school.

I went home and worked and it was just over a year before I got back down to Grambling. I had two agendas down at Grambling. One was to visit the school and the second was to keep my word to this young lady. I ended up meeting back up with Jessica during the time I was there with my father. We picked up right where we left off from our initial meetings. Things were still looking promising. After rekindling with Ms. Freshman, I decided to go to the drive-thru daiquiri shop. This is a big change from Oakland. I decided on a Caribbean daiquiri and this specific parish allowed open containers. I headed down the road to Monroe to meet back up with my father in Ms. Freshman's black Nissan Altima.

I was driving in Louisiana, a foreign place to me. I did this because my dad had already gone back to the hotel. I got to the city of Monroe I forgot what exit to get off. I spotted a Monroe cop hiding at the bottom of the hill when I went over the hill. I had a gut feeling I was going to get pulled over and there I was racially profiled as the cop pulls me over.

The cop did not even tell me I was speeding. I kept asking the police why I was pulled over. He asked me what I had in the cup. I told him I had a hurricane he told me to dump it because it is not allowed in Monroe. I poured the drink out on the road. The cop told me the reason he pulled me over was because law enforcement was worried about drugs being transported from Dallas to Atlanta. Being profiled opened my eyes to the ignorance and it made me angry. It taught me the importance of being responsible for my life, educate others, and be an excellent example of a young African American male.

Chapter 20
Corporate Blues

In the late fall of 2008, I started working at a company which specialized in diabetes medication. I earned this job by going to a temp-agency. My job title was government phone specialist. I made phone calls to Veteran Affairs hospitals and coordinate shipment of diabetic supplies to the hospitals to make sure each hospital was fully stocked.

I was supplied with my computer and monitor from the technology department. The whole facility was operated like a fortress. There were cameras all around the facility. The parking lot and every entry and exit point of the building had a camera. There were two of us that worked as a specialist. A Cuban gentleman from Florida was my co-worker. I was doing a great job. About a month into the job, I got to work at 4:00 in the morning. When I arrived at my desk, my computer was missing.

I called my manager to let him know what happened. He asks me if I was sure the computer was gone. I went to the security personnel director to report the computer stolen. I asked him to look at the cameras to determine where my computer went. He explained he was not able to pull the footage. The incident had to be an inside job. Of course, I did not take the computer. The initial reaction by my manager was that I took it. That was not the case. I assured my manager that I had no need for a computer and that's why I immediately went to security to try to help resolve the case immediately. It did not feel good to be questioned about a computer I did not take. I don't know whatever came of it. I assumed they figured it out because I kept my job and moved on from it.

It is always important to watch your surroundings. As I mentioned previously, report things immediately if you see something wrong. Be careful who you associate with, even at work. You never know who may be out to sabotage your reputation. It can sometimes feel like you are at war with hidden traps and tactics in some corporate settings. Stay close to God and always pray.

In 2013, I was driving home from work around 10:30 in the morning. I was driving through a town called Orinda. It's a small town and they are known for speed traps on San Pablo Dam Road. I am always cautious driving through there and watch my driving speed because you just never know when the cops are lurking to pull you over. They are just a security type of police department that just does

117

not have much to do. Anyone African American, young or old can be susceptible to being profiled anywhere in the United States.

On a different day, I was headed to work driving through the town of Orinda. I was driving about thirty miles per hour. I have practiced this so many times in the past because I can usually feel when a cop is nearby. I reminded myself to stay calm, focus, look ahead, and think about God. I happened to be on the phone with my buddy Marcus this particular day but I got off the phone. The speed trap is usually about two miles long.

I made it through successfully. I thought once I made it through the thirty miles per hour zone and went through the light, the speed limit would go up to forty-five miles per hour. Usually, the cops would turn around once they got to that point but this particular day, he continued to trail me. I kept my car under the speed limit and the cop followed me another couple miles. I stayed focused and kept God on my mind. The cop turned into a nearby parking lot and I didn't have any issues. It is such a shame in today's time, many blacks are still being profiled. Always stay calm in these types of situations and keep God first.

Chapter 21

A Letter to the Visionaries

In our society, some have attained an element of achievement in our community. Others have careers and a few extra dollars to spare. We focus on pulling ourselves up by our bootstraps. America glorifies the triumphant person who started at the bottom and excelled to the top. Society has molded individualism to the point of poison, where husband and wife fight over money and some women choose career over love and working as a team. Working as a team gets us where we need to go.

It is disheartening that some of our HBCU's have gone underfunded and undesirable when there is so much economic clout in our community. Many of us spend thousands of dollars at hotels and at annual festivals and don't consider giving a small portion back to help our alma maters. We spend millions of dollars on hotels from Atlanta to Las Vegas to Orlando at conventions. An economic strategy can help develop a lasting legacy. Quit spending our money in places where they do not care about our interests.

Everyone is concerned about where their money is going. We should help out and understand it is not just the black colleges that need help. We need fields and recreation centers for our youth. We need to

start thinking collectively about how we can help motivate one another

to own companies. The future is up to us.

Conclusion

I pray after you have read this book, you feel inspired by it. This story is for my black men. It is for our community, the leaders who have paved the way, those who passed away, and those who are striving to be good men, fathers, uncles, attorneys, activists, teachers, and psychologists. We salute you. I want my fellow brothers to feel their strength with my stories. It can be done as we strive and make good decisions.

To my single mothers, use this book as your compass to guide your young sons in the direction of success. You can do it. Even if you live in the underappreciated part of town, you can make it. Black men are the leaders of this generation. We must be strong for one another.

Never stop helping your community. Too many people have died for us to be apathetic. Tell your story. Make a positive difference. Fight for the cause you are passionate about. Never forget where you came from. Take time to reflect on your life and leave a legacy for others. God bless you. The future is in your mind and hands.

Acknowledgments

I would like to thank God, my Father. I'd also like to thank and acknowledge my grandparents who have all transitioned, Bill and Jessie Sharp, Grandma Thibeaux, Eugene and Leatrice McClendon. I have always had unconditional support from my mother Trinail McClendon and my father, Steve McClendon. Hats off to my late Uncle Tarmel Coleman. Much love to my Uncle Harold who lived to be 100 and Aunt Jewel who lived to be 99 years old because they were so supportive of my life. Uncle Wildon Thibeaux was a boss.

To my best friend Marcus Salem, thank you for over two decades of friendship. Rest in Peace to all the role models and business leaders in Oakland who helped shape my life. Chauncey Bailey who was an inspiring journalist. May his soul be at peace. Gary Bell supported my efforts every year for Team Cali. Mr. Bassette, my history teacher who lit my passion for reading and not being afraid to question things that aren't right. Ken Jones, a great counselor who inspired me to strive for excellence while in junior high School.

To all the music artists in Oakland and the bay area who motivated me. To all the athletes who inspired me to play sports, thank you. To Coach Raven who always said the same quote but somehow it motivated us to win games. The Potters House and Bishop TD Jakes, you have helped eradicate generational curses in the Thibeaux household. To my wife, Melissa, who has given me unwavering support. I love you.